CW00832716

Arcola Th
Ellie Keel Productions present

Anna Bella Eema

a ghost story for three bodies
with three voices

By Lisa D'Amour

Music by Chris Sidorfsky

First British performance
at the Arcola Theatre, London,
on 11 September 2019.

Anna Bella Eema

by Lisa D'Amour

ONE (Irene and others)
Beverly Rudd

TWO (Annabella and others)
Gabrielle Brooks

THREE (Anna Bella Eema and others)
Natasha Cottriall

Original Score	**Chris Sidorfsky**
Director	**Jessica Lazar**
Musical Director, Sound Designer, Additional Music	**Tom Foskett-Barnes**
Movement Director	**Jennifer Fletcher**
Assistant Director *via The King's Head Theatre TRD Scheme*	**Amber Sinclair-Case**
Set & Costume Designer	**Anna Lewis**
Lighting Designer	**David Doyle**
Production Manager	**John Rowland**
Stage Manager	**Catriona McHugh**
Accent Coach	**Carter Bellaimey**
Publicist	**Kate Morley PR**
Playwright's Agent	**George Lane at CAA**

Co-Producers
Arcola Theatre, Atticist, and Ellie Keel Productions
(Ellie Keel, Gabrielle Leadbeater, Jennifer Lunn).

Atticist would also like to thank Bridie Bischoff,
Tommo Fowler and Dr Emily Garside for their advice
and input during the production process.

Cast

Beverly Rudd | One

Beverly trained at LAMDA. Her theatre credits include *Dead Dog in a Suitcase* (Kneehigh – UK and international tour); *Brief Encounter* (Kneehigh – Lowry and Haymarket Empire Cinema); *The Tin Drum* (Kneehigh – UK tour); *The Twits* (Curve Theatre); *Peter Pan*, *The Beggar's Opera*, and *Into the Woods* (Regent's Park Open Air Theatre); *James and the Giant Peach* (West Yorkshire Playhouse); *Much Ado About Nothing* (Royal Exchange, Manchester); *Soho Cinders* (Soho Theatre); *The Little Mermaid* (Bristol Old Vic); *Acorn Antiques* (Phil McIntyre Productions); *Girls Just Want to Have* Fun (Limelight Entertainment/Fiery Angel); *The Magistrate* (National Theatre); *Brief Encounter* (Kneehigh No 1 tour); *Days of Significance* (RSC/Tricycle Theatre); *Titus Andronicus* (Paradoxos Theatre); *The Hole Story* (Paines Plough).

Television credits include: *Trollied* Seasons 1–7 – Series Regular Lisa (Roughcut/Sky); *Oodleooos* (CBBC); *The Function Room* (Zeppotron/Channel 4); *Coronation Street* (ITV); *Shameless* (Channel 4); *Him and Her*, *Inn Mates* and *Scallywagga* (all BBC3); *Guantanamo Phil* (BBC); *Octavia* (Touchpaper); *No Angels* (World Productions/Channel 4).

Film credits include: *Mad, Bad and Sad* (Moxie 1 Ltd) and *Service* (IWC Media).

Beverly's awards include the RTS Award for Best Performance in a Comedy 2009 (for *Massive*).

Gabrielle Brooks | Two

Gabrielle's theatre credits include: *A Midsummer Night's Dream* (Regent's Park Open Air Theatre); *Twelfth Night* (Young Vic); *Our Lady of Kibeho* (Royal & Derngate, Northampton); *The Way of the World* (Donmar Warehouse); *The Wizard of Oz* and *Everybody's Talking About Jamie* (Sheffield Crucible); *Queen Anne* (RSC/Theatre Royal Haymarket); *Lazarus* (King's Cross Theatre); *The Stranger's Case* (Liverpool Everyman); *The Book of Mormon* (Prince of Wales Theatre); *I Can't Sing* (London Palladium); *Our House 10th Anniversary* (Savoy Theatre); *Avenue* Q and *Hairspray* (UK tours); *Synergy Play Readings* (Theatre 503); *Red Snapper* (Belgrade Theatre, Coventry).

Radio credits include: *Passenger List Podcast* (Panoply); *Nicked* (BBC Radio 4); *Enna Gee* (CBeebies Radio).

Television credits include: *Coming Down the Mountain* and *Grange Hill* (BBC).

Film credits include: *Notes on a Scandal* (Fox Searchlight Pictures).

Natasha Cottriall | Three

Natasha trained at Mountview Academy.

Her theatre credits include: *Hairspray* (Gordon Craig Theatre); *Dancing in the Streets* (UK tour); *Future Conditional* (Old Vic); Little Red Riding Hood in *Into the Woods* (Royal Exchange, Manchester); *The Busker's Opera* (Park Theatre); *Here Lie the Remains of Mercy* (Theatre Delicatessen); *Beautiful – The Carole King Musical* (Aldwych Theatre); Mary Lennox in *The Secret Garden* (Theatre by the Lake); *The Selfish Giant* (Vaudeville Theatre); Ado Annie in *Oklahoma!* (Grange Park Opera); Ruth Connor/Buckley Salmon in the world premiere of *The Lovely Bones*, adapted by Bryony Lavery (UK tour). Most recently, she appeared as Felicity Dangle in *Whodunnit Unrehearsed* (Park Theatre).

Television credits include: Claudette in *Grantchester* (ITV); Rosie Griffiths (semi-regular) in *Doctors* (BBC1); Amelia Garwood in *Vera* Series 9 (ITV).

Film includes: *Aladdin* (Disney).

Creative Team

Lisa D'Amour | Writer

Lisa D'Amour is a playwright and co-artistic director of PearlDamour, a genre-defying performance company. Her plays have been produced on Broadway at Manhattan Theater Club's Samuel J. Friedman Theater, Playwrights Horizons (NYC), Steppenwolf Theater (Chicago), The Wilma Theater (Philadelphia), Woolly Mammoth (Washington DC), the National Theatre (London), Southern Rep (New Orleans) and many other theatres across the globe. PearlDamour creates interdisciplinary, often site-specific works which range from the intimate to large scale, including *How to Build a Forest* – an eight-hour performance in which PearlDamour builds a majestic, fabricated forest by hand – and *Lost in the Meadow*, a performance made for the forty-acre Meadow in Longwood Botanical Gardens, created with set designer Mimi Lien. Lisa's play *Detroit* was a finalist for both the Pulitzer Prize for Drama and the Susan Smith Blackburn Prize and won the OBIE Award for Best New American Play. She is a past recipient of the Alpert Award for the Arts, the Steinberg Playwright Award, and is a 2013 Doris Duke Artist. Lisa is an alumnae of playwright residences at New Dramatists and the Playwrights' Center.

Chris Sidorfsky | Composer

Chris is a US-based composer. He holds a BA in Music from Macalester College and an MFA in Musical Theatre Writing from New York University.

Jessica Lazar | Director

Jessica Lazar is a freelance director and a co-founder of Atticist. She is currently an EVOLVE Artist in Residence at Oxford Playhouse. Her productions have won the 2016 Carol Tambor Best of Edinburgh Award and the inaugural 2018 SIT-Up Award (for 'social impact theatre'), and been nominated for several Off West End Awards including Best Director, Best Ensemble, and Best Production. Theatre credits include: Katherine Rundell's *Life According to Saki* (Edinburgh Fringe, 2016/ Fourth Street Theatre New York, 2017), Nazish Khan's *Deadly Dialogues* (Edinburgh Fringe/3LD New York, 2017), Steven Berkoff's *East* (King's Head Theatre, 2018), Christina Murdock's *Dangerous Giant Animals* (Edinburgh Fringe/United Solo Fest New York/Park Theatre, 2018), David Greig's *Outlying Islands* (King's Head, 2019), Sam Potter's *The Unicorn* and Iman Qureshi's *This is a Love Story* (North Wall, 2019). In 2016, she completed an AHRC-funded doctorate under Professor Tiffany Stern, then Professor of Drama at Oxford University.

Tom Foskett-Barnes | Music Director, Sound Designer & Additional Music

Tom Foskett-Barnes is a London-based composer for film and theatre. Film credits include the Academy Award-nominated *Black Sheep* (dir. Ed Perkins, 2017), *Four Quartets* (dir. Marco Alessi, 2017, Berlin International Film Festival, Special Mention from the Crystal Bear Jury), and *toni_with_an_i* (dir. Marco Alessi, BBC4). For stage, Tom has composed and served as musical director for productions of *Pufferfish* (VAULT Festival), *Treasure Island* (Arts Ed), *Twelfth Night* and *Othello* (Leicester Square Theatre), *All's Well That Ends Well* and *The Two Gentleman of Verona* (Changeling Theatre).

In 2016 Tom was Sound and Music Composer in Residence with ROLI as part of the Embedded_Innovate Scheme. The residency culminated with the screening of MIDWAY, an audio-visual work about the residents of a council estate. Tom was selected as part of the Old Vic 12 in 2017. During the residency Tom composed music for *One Voice* (dir. Annabel Bolton) and was Musical Supervisor for *The Greatest Wealth* (dir. Adrian Lester), both staged at the Old Vic. In 2019 Tom completed *Living with the Light On: Switchboard since the 70s*, an audio documentary about the LGBT+ charity Switchboard. The work was commissioned by the Institute of Contemporary Art as part of the New Creatives programme and will be broadcast by the BBC.

Tom trained at the Royal College of Music as a Soirée d'Or Scholar generously supported by a Clifton Parker Award and was also the recipient of a BAFTA UK Scholarship. Tom is a participant in the 2019 BFI NETWORK x BAFTA Crew programme.

Jennifer Fletcher | Movement Director

Jennifer trained in Dance Theatre at Laban and takes on multiple creative roles for theatre, opera and film productions. Theatre credits as Choreographer include: *Much Ado About Nothing* and *The Tempest* (Grosvenor Park Open Air Theatre); *As Long as the Heart Beats*

(National Theatre Wales); *The Secret Seven* (Storyhouse); *Rapunzel* (Cambridge Junction); *Thor & Loki* (Vicky Graham Productions/Harry Blake); *The Beggar's Opera* (Storyhouse); *Outlying Islands* (Atticist); *Jason and the Argonauts* (Unicorn Theatre); *Dido and Aeneas* (Bath International Festival/RCM); *The Snow Child* (Unicorn Theatre/ Sheffield Theatre); *People of the Eye* and *Mathilda and the Orange Balloon* (Deaf & Hearing Ensemble) .

As a Writer/Director, Jennifer recently collaborated with Harry Blake to create the new musical *The Sandman*, supported by the Andrew Lloyd Webber Foundation and BRIT school (Southwark Playhouse). She was the Associate Director for *Semele* (Mid Wales Opera/RWCMD) and *Don Giovanni* (Longborough Festival Opera), and continues to direct work internationally for the two companies she co-founded: The Mostly Everything People and NOVA. Both work with multiple disciplines and methods of combining text, movement, live music and language.

Anna Lewis | Set & Costume Designer

Anna is an award-winning set and costume designer. She was a Jerwood Young Designer 2016/17 and a recipient of the MGC Futures bursary.

Her previous design work with Atticist includes *Outlying Islands* (King's Head Theatre – Offie-nominated for Best Production), *EAST* (King's Head Theatre), and *Life According to Saki* (Edinburgh Fringe – Winner of the Carol Tambour Best of Edinburgh Award, subsequently transferred Off Broadway). Other theatre credits include *Carmen* (King's Head Theatre), *Dangerous Giant Animals* (Edinburgh Fringe - Winner of the SIT-Up Award, VAULT Festival), *A New Coat for Christmas* (Oxford Playhouse/Reading Rep), *After October* (Finborough Theatre – Offie-nominated for Best Costume Design) and *Deadly Dialogues* (Edinburgh Festival, 3LD, New York).

Anna was Lead Costume Supervisor for Turner Prize winner Jeremy Deller's multi-award-winning *we're here because we're here* - a living memorial to those who lost their lives on the first day of the Somme (National Theatre, 2016). This involved coordinating with 27 theatres nationally and responsibility for over 2000 costumes. As an Associate, Anna has worked at The Gate and The Bush. She was the Costume Assistant on the multi-award-winning *The Inheritance* (Young Vic, Noel Coward Theatre) and has worked extensively in the Props Department at the National Theatre. Earlier this year she was the Costume Assistant for Christopher Wheeldon's *Cinderella* at the Royal Albert Hall and she is currently working on *The Snow Queen* for the Tivoli Ballet Company designed by HM Queen Margrethe of Denmark.

David Doyle | Lighting Designer

David is a freelance lighting designer working across Ireland and the UK. Previous work with Atticist includes *Life According to Saki*, which won the Carol Tambor Best of Edinburgh Award and transferred Off-Broadway in 2017, and *East* at the King's Head Theatre in 2018 for which he was nominated for an Offie for Best Lighting Design. Most recently he collaborated with Atticist on *Outlying Islands* which was nominated for an Offie for Best Production. Other recent work includes: *Carmen* (King's Head Theatre); *Brendan Galileo for Europe* (UK and Irish tour); *Richard Carpenter is Close to You* (UK and Australian tour); *Dangerous Giant Animals* (winner of the SIT-Up Award); *The Cat's Mother* (Winner of the Fishamble New Writing Award); *Confirmation* (Nominated for the Outburst Award); *My Name is Saoirse* (Winner of the Best Theatre Award at Adelaide Fringe, the First Fortnight Award, and an Argus Angel); *Substance* (Winner of the NSDF Commendation for Lighting Design). His work has been seen in venues across Europe, the USA, and Australia and has been nominated for awards including the Little Gem Award and the Judge's Choice Award at the Dublin Fringe, and the Edinburgh Award at the Edinburgh Fringe. David also works as a producer and is currently the Producing Assistant for the Abbey Theatre, Ireland's National Theatre.

Amber Sinclair-Case | Assistant Director
(King's Head TRD Scheme)

Amber recently graduated from the Musical Theatre Performance course at University of Chichester. Her recent theatre credits as Assistant Director include *Debut* (Bridewell Theatre), as well the world premiere of *The Stationmaster* (Assembly Theatre, Bognor Regis). She is on the Trainee Resident Director scheme at the King's Head Theatre, a year-long educational training programme. For more information, please visit <www.kingsheadtheatre.com/trainee-directors>.

Catriona McHugh | Stage Manager

Credits as Stage Manager include: Almeida Young Company shows, *The Wave* and (*This Isn't*) *A True Story* (Almeida Theatre), *Hoard* (Arcola Theatre), *Chasing Bono* (Soho Theatre), *Wasted* (Southwark Playhouse), *Spun* (Arcola Theatre), *Lock and Key*, *Ad Libido*, *Mary's Babies* (The Vault's Festival 18), *Talk Radio* (Old Red Lion Theatre), *Boom* (Theatre 503).

Credit for other roles: *Three Sisters* (Tech Week Runner, Almeida Theatre), *The Writer* (stage crew), *The Twilight Zone* (tech week runner, Almeida Theatre), *Albion* (Assistant Stage Manager, Almeida).

Carter Bellaimey | Accent Coach

Carter is a US-native Dialect Coach based in London. He has a BFA in Acting from Rutgers University and an MA in Sociocultural Linguistics from Goldsmiths University.

He has coached actors such as Jodie Whitaker (*Broadchurch*, *Doctor Who*), Tom Mison (*Sleepy Hollow*), Matthew Macfadyen (*Succession* HBO, *Spooks*), Alex Hassell (*Cowboy Beebop* Netflix, *Suburbicon*), and Adam Bernard (*Dream Girls* – 2017 Olivier Award for Best Supporting Actor in a Musical), as well as actors from TV series such as *Narcos*, *The Last Kingdom*, *The Get Down*, *Indian Summers*, and *The Missing*; and from theatrical productions such as *War Horse* (Lincoln Center), *London Wall* (Off-Broadway), and *Henry V* (RSC).

John Rowland | Production Manager

John has worked in London's West End on Disney's *The Lion King* (Lyceum Theatre), *We Will Rock You* (Dominion Theatre), the RSC's *Matilda the Musical* (Cambridge Theatre), worked on four Royal Variety Performances, *Cats* (London Palladium) and two of the biggest pantos in the UK – *Cinderella* and *Dick Whittington* (London Palladium).

Working in commercial UK and international touring, John has production managed on *Aladdin* (2019, Milton Keynes Theatre), *Friendsical* (2019, UK tour and Edinburgh Fringe), *Avenue Q* (2019, UK tour), *Flashdance the Musical* (2019, Korean tour), *Fame* (2018/19, UK and international tour), *Wizard of Oz* (2018, Blackpool Winter Gardens), *Flashdance the Musical* (2017/18, UK and international tour).

John started up ProdEM (Production and Event Management) in 2018, and since then ProdEM has carried out work for *Britain's Got Talent: The Champions 2019* (Wembley Arena), ITV's *British Soap Awards* (2019, Lowry Theatre Manchester), *FriendsFest* (2019 tour), BAFTA Film Awards 2019 (Royal Albert Hall), ITV's *All Star Musicals* (London Palladium), ITV's Sport Department (Royal Ascot), *West End Eurovision* (2019, Adelphi Theatre) and *Magic Mike* (Hippodrome Casino).

Ellie Keel | Producer, Ellie Keel Productions

Ellie Keel is an independent arts producer with a broad portfolio of theatre productions and events to her name. After two years working for Thelma Holt Ltd, the Oxford Playhouse, and the Cameron Mackintosh Foundation, she now specialises in commissioning and creating successful productions of new plays with her company Ellie Keel Productions. Ellie's work encompasses productions in many London off-West End venues, including Barbican Centre (*Redefining Juliet*), Soho Theatre (*HOTTER*), Arcola (*Callisto: a Queer Epic*; *Heretic Voices*; *Mrs Dalloway*; *Anna Bella Eema*), the Finborough Theatre (*Home Chat*); Theatre503 (*The Games We Played*); and VAULT Festival (*Collapsible*; *The D Word*). In 2017 she co-founded Heretic Voices, an international competition to find the best new plays in monologue form. Ellie is also a Creative Associate at the North Wall Arts Centre, where she is the co-founder of the annual Alchymy Festival, showcasing the work of talented early-career theatremakers from across the UK. In addition to her professional productions, Ellie has produced large-scale, site-specific plays with the Big House, a charity working with young people at risk of social exclusion. Ellie is a Director of LGBT+ youth charity Just Like Us and a Trustee of The King's Hall Trust for the Arts.

Gabrielle Leadbeater | Associate Producer, Ellie Keel Productions

Gabrielle is an Associate Producer with Ellie Keel Productions. In 2019, Gabrielle has worked with EKP to present a season of four shows at the Edinburgh Festival Fringe: *Collapsible* by Margaret Perry (Assembly), in co-production with HighTide; *Where to Belong* by Victor Esses (Summerhall); *Son of Dyke* by Jordan Waller; and *HOTTER* by Mary Higgins and Ell Potter (Underbelly). Her credits as an independent producer include *My Mother Runs in Zig-Zags* (North Wall Arts Centre), *Your Little Play* (Michael Pilch Studio), and *Medea* (Belgrade Theatre). Gabrielle is also a backstage member of the National Youth Theatre and her Stage Management credits include *The Reluctant Fundamentalist* (Bradford Literary Festival and the Edinburgh Fringe Festival); *Vintage New Year's Party* (Southbank Centre); *Zigger Zagger* (Wilton's Music Hall); *Twelfth Night* (Middle Temple Hall); and *The Story of Our Youth* (Shaftesbury Theatre).

Atticist

Atticist is a collaborative theatre company founded in 2016. Atticist's first production won the Carol Tambor Best of Edinburgh Award at the 2016 Edinburgh Fringe and transferred Off Broadway in 2017. Since then, Atticist has produced two further acclaimed and multi-award-nominated revivals, as well as continuing to develop new writing. Productions: Katherine Rundell's *Life According to Saki* (Edinburgh Fringe/Fourth Street Theatre, NYC – Winner of the Carol Tambor Award 2016); Steven Berkoff's *East* (King's Head Theatre – nominations included Finalist for Off West End Award Best Ensemble 2018); David Greig's *Outlying Islands* (King's Head Theatre – current Nominee for Off West End Award Best Production 2019), and the 2019 Alchymy Monologues in association with North Wall Arts Centre, Oxford: Iman Qureshi's *This is a Love Story*, and Sam Potter's *The Unicorn*.

Ellie Keel Productions

Ellie Keel Productions is an award-winning company producing new theatre shows in London, Edinburgh, and on tour. In 2019, EKP presented a season of four shows at the Edinburgh Festival Fringe: *Collapsible* by Margaret Perry, in co-production with HighTide (Assembly); *Where to Belong* by Victor Esses (Summerhall); *Son of Dyke* by Jordan Waller; and *HOTTER* by Mary Higgins and Ell Potter (Underbelly).

arcola
theatre

Arcola produces daring, high-quality theatre in the heart of East London and beyond.

We commission and premiere exciting, original works alongside rare gems of world drama and bold new productions of classics.

Our socially-engaged, international programme champions diversity, challenges the status quo, and attracts over 65,000 people to our building each year. Ticket prices are some of the most affordable in London, and our long-running Pay What You Can scheme ensures there is no financial barrier to accessing the theatre.

Every year, we offer 26 weeks of free rehearsal space to BAME and refugee artists; our Grimeborn Festival opens up opera with contemporary stagings at affordable prices; and our Participation department creates over 13,500 creative opportunities for the people of Hackney and beyond. Our pioneering environmental initiatives are award-winning, and aim to make Arcola the world's first carbon-neutral theatre.

Game Changers
Graham and Christine Benson, Roger Bradburn & Helen Main, Andrew Cripps, Robert Fowler, Daniel Friel, David Alan & Jean Grier, Sarah Morrison, Rosie Schumm

Trailblazers
Katie Bradford, Catrin Evans, Gold Family, Jon Gilmartin, Stuart Honey, Melanie Johnson, Katrin Maeurich

www.arcolatheatre.com   020 7503 1646

Artistic Director
Mehmet Ergen

Executive Producer
Leyla Nazli

Executive Director
Ben Todd

Associate Director
Jack Gamble

Producer
Richard Speir

Assistant Producer
Emma Attwell

New Work Assistant
Eleanor Dawson

Finance & Operations

Operations Manager
Natalja Derendiajeva

Finance Manager
Steve Haygreen

Finance Assistant
Marcela Royas

IT Manager and Software Developer
Nick Cripps

IT Assistant and Software Developer
Oliver Brill

Health and Safety Manager
Charlotte Croft

Health and Safety Assistant
Miriam Mahony

Sustainability Assistant
Helen Freudenberg

Front of House

Front of House & Box Office Manager
Norna Yau

Front of House & Box Office
Assistant Manager &
Access Development Manager
James York

Front of House Supervisors
Emily Jones, Mary Roubos

Participation

Participation Manager
Bec Martin-Williams

Participation Coordinator
Rach Skyer

Production

Head of Production
Geoff Hense

Chief Technician
Michael Paget

For a full staff list, see
www.arcolatheatre.com

MAKE THIS HAPPEN

Text **ARCO14 £3** to 70070
to give £3 in support of Arcola

Standard network charges apply.

Director's Note on *Anna Bella Eema*

In a rundown trailer in a deserted trailer park, a girl called Annabella lives alone with her eccentric and imaginative mother, Irene. There used to be others: a community full of women and children existing just beyond the mainstream, managing the wild and the weird as well as the everyday together. But the construction of an Interstate has closed the park. Only Annabella and Irene remain and, although their protest seems futile, Irene will not give up her home. So Annabella – lonely, frustrated, and growing up fast – builds a girl out of mud. The girl comes to life. They name her Anna Bella Eema. And she will not let Irene and Annabella shut out the coming changes any more.

Who is Anna Bella Eema? She has aspects of the mythical Golem (a clay person brought to life by magic, often to defend a community under threat), but also of a *genius loci* (a protective spirit linked to a particular place). In the characters' dreams she appears as a hyena, a cat, a fox, all of which have mythological roles as shapeshifting tricksters. Mostly, however, she appears more-or-less human, and imbued with Annabella's adolescent desire and defiance, Irene's glorious imagination and occasional fear. Only Irene and Annabella ever see her.

The play conjures a world of amber light and drowsy humid heat, where the supernatural is part of the everyday. Construction sites house vampires and the nearby woods are full of monsters. There is music on the air and endless storytelling. Like its characters, *Anna Bella Eema* is born of a specific place. This is the southern United States, maybe (though we are never told this) Lisa D'Amour's Louisiana on the disappearing shores of the expanding Gulf. It is a Southern Gothic tale, and not just because of the key genre elements of location, unconventional protagonists tussling with society, and flair for the uncanny and supernatural. According to Tennessee Williams, Southern Gothic also displays 'a sense, an intuition, of an underlying dreadfulness in modern experience'; in particular, others add, it shows 'an almost unbearable anxiety about [the] costs' of 'progress'. And it warns that repressed or othered elements of a person, nation, or culture will arise to confront and transform its present – for good and bad.*

All these elements can be found here. *Anna Bella Eema* is about growing up, growing older, and learning to survive. It is about aspiration and desire, and the unease that stalks them. It is about mental health, power, and resistance; about the environment and about place. But, unlike much Southern Gothic, it is also strangely encouraging. When *Anna Bella Eema* considers the inevitability of change and loss, it also sees the possibility of transformation and discovery; that the lost things have made us who we are. It praises individuality but also belonging; it speaks of the desire to claim one's own story, but also to share that story with others. For every moment it dwells on extinction, it offers as much time to creation.

We will never know what the mud girl really is. Instead *Anna Bella Eema* offers us space to dwell in possibility and, in doing so, makes us consider what we value. What transformation are we facing — or perhaps seeking to ignore? What sacrifices will it demand? What things, lying in its path, will we defend against almost inevitable defeat? *Anna Bella Eema* repeatedly asks its characters to 'wake up' to the changing world around them and to face it with courage and imagination. It is urging us to do the same.

Jessica Lazar
August 2019

Anna Bella Eema

Lisa D'Amour is a playwright and co-artistic director of PearlDamour, a genre-defying performance company. Her plays have been produced on Broadway at Manhattan Theater Club's Samuel J. Friedman Theater, Playwrights Horizons (NYC), Steppenwolf Theater (Chicago), The Wilma Theater (Philadelphia), Woolly Mammoth (Washington DC), National Theatre (London), Southern Rep (New Orleans) and many other theatres across the globe. PearlDamour creates interdisciplinary, often site-specific works which range from the intimate to large scale, including *How to Build a Forest* – an eight-hour performance in which PearlDamour builds a majestic, fabricated forest by hand – and *Lost in the Meadow*, a performance made for the forty-acre Meadow in Longwood Botanical Gardens, created with set designer Mimi Lien. Lisa's play *Detroit* was a finalist for both the Pulitzer Prize for Drama and the Susan Smith Blackburn Prize and won the OBIE Award for Best New American Play. She is a past recipient of the Alpert Award for the Arts, the Steinberg Playwright Award, and is a 2013 Doris Duke Artist. Lisa is an alumnae of playwright residences at New Dramatists and the Playwrights' Center.

also by Lisa D'Amour from Faber

DETROIT

LISA D'AMOUR

Anna Bella Eema

*a ghost story for three bodies
with three voices*

FABER & FABER

First published in the USA by Playscripts, Inc, New York, 2003

First published in this revised version, 2019
by Faber and Faber Limited
74–77 Great Russell Street
London WC1B 3DA

Typeset by Country Setting, Kingsdown, Kent CT14 8ES
Printed in England by CPI Group (UK) Ltd, Croydon CRO 4YY

A CIP record for this book is available from the British Library

ISBN 978-0-571-35635-5

2 4 6 8 10 9 7 5 3 1

Introduction

Sometimes plays are born from two thoughts that drop randomly into a writer's head, and align. This early work, *Anna Bella Eema*, began when my passing knowledge of the Jewish Golem myth – a Rabbi makes a man out of mud – bumped up against a local news story about an impoverished woman living in a trailer home whose children were taken from her by Child Protective Services.

Growing up Catholic, I was always drawn to mysticism and ritual. I found the Golem myth entrancing, but I was overwhelmed by its masculinity.

The tone of the news story startled me, drenched as it was in entitled judgement. A male reporter, speaking sternly. The trailer home was derelict; the monster mother responsible for both her own offspring and her sister's. No running water or electricity. Children at risk of dehydration and neglect.

Then the reporter let the woman speak. She was well-kept, and weeping. She was short on cash, and her sister was very sick. She was doing the best she could. She was getting water from her neighbour and pouring it in the toilet, and keeping some for dishes. She hoped to have the money to turn on the electricity soon.

Where did the truth lie? In the reporter or the woman?

I sat down to write: trailer home, single mom in crisis, girl made from mud by a girl. Early attempts to write this as a box-set, realistic play failed quickly. This story wanted prismatic perspective. I let the single mother,

Irene, start speaking, then realised she was speaking directly to the audience, then that she wanted to sing. The form of the play – a spoken and sung ghost story – grew organically from Irene's opening words. The music by Chris Sidorfsky helped to theatricalize Irene's inner life, her fierce survival instincts and those of her daughter, Annabella.

Anna Bella Eema was first produced eighteen years ago, in a warehouse theatre space in Austin, Texas, in 2001, and then in 2003 in a 100-seat black box in downtown New York. Since then, it has been produced in dozens of fierce, experimental theatres across the US. I love that this play has provided challenging roles to virtuosic actresses living in cities of many sizes throughout my country.

I was thrilled when Jessica Lazar and Atticist Theatre approached me about a London production at the Arcola. I was moved by their enthusiasm for the work, and energised by Atticist's stellar reputation for close collaborations with playwrights on revival. I asked Jessica if she would be up for me doing a bit of work on the script. I felt there was some reframing needed, since the world has become dominated by screens and the internet, and I wanted to revisit one dastardly section that I could never get quite right (there's always one, isn't there?)

I'm grateful to Atticist and Faber & Faber for letting me stay in process with this piece, even after all these years. Here's to more stories about growth, change, and conjuring strength and resilience out of the dirt.

Lisa D'Amour, August 2019

Author's Notes

Anna Bella Eema is written for three actresses sitting in three chairs.

In performance, spoken word shifts suddenly into sung aria, ambient soundscapes shift into the voice of a character.

A swift-changing sound world is essential to the movement of the piece. Sound moves about in this play as actors move about in others, and the progression of melody and rhythm helps support the shifting points of view of the story.

I ask the reader to try and hear, to the best of his/her/ their imaginative ability, these different sound textures.

There are three optional cuts in the piece [indicated by square brackets, thus].

ACKNOWLEDGEMENTS

Some of the text was inspired by the book *Wild Animals I Have Known* by Ernest Thompson Seton.

Certain aspects of the oratory style were inspired by Cecil Michael's *Round Trip to Hell in a Flying Saucer*. Thanks to Mr Michael for his unabashed belief in the supernatural and his ardent need write it down.

Many thanks to the Playwrights' Center, New Dramatists, and Nautilus Music Theater for helping me develop this play.

Anna Bella Eema, in a co-production with Atticist Productions and Ellie Keel Productions, received its first British performance at the Arcola Theatre, London, on 11 September 2019. The cast was as follows:

One Beverly Rudd
Two Gabrielle Brooks
Three Natasha Cottriall

Director Jessica Lazar
Music Director and Sound Designer
  Tom Foskett-Barnes
Original Score Chris Sidorfsky
Designer Anna Lewis
Lighting Designer David Doyle
Movement Director Jennifer Fletcher

An early version of *Anna Bella Eema* was produced by Refraction Arts/Physical Plant Theater, Austin, Texas, in 2001, directed by Katie Pearl.

Anna Bella Eema premiered in New York City in a co-production with New Georges and HERE Arts Center in October 2003, also directed by Katie Pearl.

The present text includes revisions made for the UK premiere of the play, produced by Atticist Productions/Ellie Keel Productions at the Arcola Theatre in September 2019.

Characters

Actress One
A thick woman. Sturdy. Like Miss Amelia in
Carson McCuller's *Ballad of the Sad Café*.
She has stayed put, like a tree, for most of her life.
She has a strong, deep voice: her roots reach deep
into the earth, searching for the water that might
bring her back to life.

Actress Two
Impish. Eyes that sparkle and a voice that reaches
towards the sky: it loops, stretches and rockets.
She is ready to blaze on out of here.

Actress Three
Also impish. Sometimes she seems like Actress Two's
twin sister. Until we glimpse her mischievous,
supernatural soul.

Three actresses sit in three chairs, facing the audience. The actress sitting in the middle, Actress One, sits a little closer to the audience than Two and Three, so the three women form a triangle.

Each actress has an old, rusty TV tray in front of them. Each TV tray is carefully set with kitchen tools, books, tape recorders, glass bottles and other random objects.

As the audience gathers, the actresses are 'tuning up': finding sounds in the objects on the trays, setting the objects in the correct places, warming up their voices. Eventually, the actresses sing a little ditty, a round, a prelude to the play.

One, Two *and* **Three**
    Mud girl, mud girl
    Six little fingers and six long toes
    See the mud girl
    Climb up the trellis
    To peer in the window
    Munching on a rose
    Mud girl, munch.

Actress One looks the audience in the eye, and begins to speak.

One My name is Irene and I have been alive here in this trailer home for as long as I can remember. When you are alive in one space for such a long time, the things that you remember mix with the things that are happening now, and the things that you dream about. What I mean is, sometimes the things that are happening are equal to the things that are not happening. So, as I speak to you, please do not ask me to come clear on such points as 'happened', 'did not happen', 'is happening', 'will happen'. They are all simmering in one pot. Here on the electric radar range inside this trailer home.

You can see I am a thick woman. Look at my wrist. One time someone tried to poke a stick through this wrist, in order to pin it to the ground. They poked and poked and poked, but the stick would not go through. The scar is long gone, as you can see. [This kind of thickness goes for the rest of my body too. Look at my ankle. Look at my waist.]

Here is the time line of my life. Birth. Learn to talk. Learn to read a little. Learn to love. Learn to walk (yes, very late). Father is leaving. Learn to watch my mother smash bottles. I am gaining weight. Go to school. Math. Learn how to not get made fun of. Camping out with the kids in the trailer park. Learn how not to love too much. Pull the thick braids of the rich girls. He is smiling at me. Darkness and breathing in dust. Mother, I feel a bird fluttering. I am having a baby. Look at her beautiful teeth! I am fifteen and then now I am twenty-five.

One considers the audience.

Here we are.

I was visited by a werewolf once. The werewolf said to me: 'The life of a wild animal always has a tragic end.' He took out his fangs (fake fangs! I exclaimed), laid them on the table, threw his knapsack over his shoulder and left. Here are the fangs.

She takes out a pair of fake fangs and places them on her tray.

I want to tell you the story of my girl, and the time she made her own girl out of the plain mud right here in this trailer park, and how my girl's girl helped me face certain forces slouching closer and closer to this trailer home, and how this chain of events led to my girl to becoming the girl she is today.

Right now I am taking you to the pull-out couch. This is how we sleep here in the trailer home. There is a small bedroom over on the other side of the home, off the kitchen. But you cannot see the TV so well from there. At night, me and my daughter pull out the pull-out couch and get in to watch TV. When we get in, the pull-out couch squeaks like so.

Two does a startlingly good imitation of a pull-out couch squeaking.

We try not to move too much so we can hear what the TV has to say. Once we fall asleep, I hear my daughter say:

One, Two *and* **Three** (*a dissonant trio*)
     You are so thick, Mother!
     So like a tree thick rings
     circle round your heart
     I cannot feel you breathe
     you are so thick, Mother
     Mother do you breathe?

Three makes the noise of TV static.

One I pop awake and she's asleep and I see the TV hissing at me so I turn it off.

Three stops.

She is breathing heavy on the pull-out couch and grinding her teeth. I know I'll never get to sleep so I walk to the window and open it. The full moon is out. I look at it and think about how I never really tried to get out of the trailer park. This was the trailer park I grew up in. Some people call these mobile homes. In order to make it mobile you need wheels and I don't have wheels. You will notice that my mobile home sits upon eight regular cinder blocks, with extra plywood covering for protection.

This is what my daughter is like in the mornings: impish. She lies in the bed like she's talking in her sleep: the same creepy spells over and over.

Two (*sings*)
    Who shot the La La
    I don't know
    Who shot the La La
    I don't know
    Who shot the La La
    I don't know
    I think it was a 44.

One When I do get her up, she bounces on the pull-out couch like it was a motel room bed.

Three makes bedspring noises.

Get down.

Two No!

One Your feet are dirty.

Two It's exercise.

One You shouldn't grind your teeth.

Two My teeth are STRONG!

One The good days are when she stops and the bad days are when her head bursts into flames while she laughs and leaps laughs and leaps, throwing the fireballs in my eyes and turning the trailer home into a regular smokehouse.

I was visited by a social worker once, and I lied and said we left the ribs in the oven for too long. She said, 'Ribs belong on a grill, ma'am.' I thanked her politely for the tip and she didn't come back.

This is what I think about the world.

Two and Three back her up: this is One's aria.

I don't much like it. Some people take to flying off to
foreign lands, find the one perfect spot in the hopes that
they might find themselves. Me, I keep the circumference
of my life small. I lick stamps for a living. My girl gets
home schooled. I have many books.

*Pause in aria as all three women dump out large sacks
filled with books.*

I have many books and I lick stamps for a living. The same
thing over and over. Some people call this monotonous.
These are the same people who spend their time flying
off to foreign lands. I think of them sometimes as I lick.
Like this.

*One begins to lick stamps and stick them on a piece
of paper as she speaks.*

I wonder what kind of person would fly off to Peru?
I wonder if he has a wrinkle in his brow and pains in
the hinge of his jaw. I wonder if he likes his 'apartment'.
He lives in an 'apartment' with a wrinkle in his brow.
He knows if he can get apart from his 'apartment' he will
become complete. And so he squeezes into the small, hot
seat of an airplane. On his way to Peru.
    I wonder what kind of person would sail to Alaska.
A person with a heart two degrees hotter than normal
body heat: 100 degrees point 6. One day my girl will sail
to Alaska.
    I wonder what kind of person would take a train to
Indianapolis.

All music stops.

I draw a blank.
    These are the things I think of as I lick: the peculiarities
of two-footed creatures that plod upright upon this earth
outside the circumference of this trailer park. I spy them
with my hawk's eye high –

One shows us her eye.

I have many things to say.

On the day my little girl made a girl, the temperature was 91 degrees at sunrise. The trailer home felt like the inside of a wolf's mouth. My girl skipped her bed-jumping, brushed her white teeth and started talking something like this:

Two (*sings*)
    The hens have been disappearing for over a month
       now, Mother
    And the trailer homes too.
    The air is as thick as your skin these days,
    the machines so loud I can't play jacks or even
       hopscotch.
    It's all coming to an end, Mother
    I can feel it in the back of my throat
    Is there anywhere we can go, Mother?
    In or out or up?
    Is there anything we can make, Mother?
    From a broomstick or a cup?
    The hens are disappearing, Mother
    the coon, the owl, the fox
    The hens have disappeared, Mother
    wake up, wake up, wake up!

One My mouth is sealed shut, perhaps from the glue of the stamps, perhaps from the knowledge that it is best not to respond to such foolishness. She is stomping on the floor. She is waving postmarked letters before my eyes. She is dancing a queer dance to get my attention. She is breaking a glass.

    She went out the door.

One holds up a broken glass.

This is the glass she broke on the morning my girl made a girl. I did not go to the window. But I could hear her hoary spell.

Two and Three whisper 'Who Shot the La La' under the following speech.

I tried to stick to my job but she was loud. I was hot. She was singing and singing and singing. My heart is beating twice the number of its normal beats. What more does she want me to do? I am not a lady with an airplane or even a fancy pair of shoes. I am well-read enough that I can teach her the things that need to be taught. I am offering you all I have, I have read you every book I own. I am feeding you straight from the vein now, I feed you what is left of my soul. Do you want to destroy me? She wants to destroy me. How can I ever teach you the things that need to be taught? I want to destroy you and leave you and never come back!

The whispering stops.

When she came back inside, she had another girl with her.

Two (*out of breath*) Mother! Mother, it's a girl!

One I felt I could not look at this second poor girl, but I did. I noticed she had mud on her fingernails. Then I noticed she had mud rubbed into the crook in her arm. Then I noticed she had mud pressed into the hollow of her collarbone. And in the creases of her face as she smiled.
    She is smiling at me.
    She was a filthy little thing. She crossed to my table and sat down as though it was her own table,
    That is the table I use for licking stamps. That is the table I use for licking stamps.

Two Maybe she will eat.

Two places an apple on her table.

Eat.

One She would not eat.

Two Maybe she will write.

Two places pen and paper on the table.

Write.

One She would not write.

Two Maybe she is deaf. HELLO!

Three cringes, covering her ears.

One She could hear.

Two WHERE-DO-YOU-COME-FROM!

One My girl started yelling.

Two WHERE-DID-YOU-COME-FROM! WHERE-DID-YOU-COME-FROM!

One And she took my girl's face in one of her hands and drew my girl's face to her face.
And she took my face in one of her hands, and drew my face to her face. We were face to face to face. The new girl was the only one breathing.
Annabella.

Two Yes, Ma.

One Is there soap in the vanity?

Two Yes, Ma.

One Take her in the washroom and clean her.

I can hear them in the bathroom.

From Two and Three: whispering. Laughing. Crying. Slapping. A Cat fight. Whispering. Howling. Whispering. Wrestling. Laughing. Screaming. Whispering.

They come out and I see that they are *both* dirty. My Annabella is holding her ear like it's been bit.

Two She doesn't come clean.

One I am about to say something when my Annabella looks me in the eye and says, a second time.

Two She doesn't come clean.

One My girl's name is Annabella and she wanted to name her girl Annabella too. I told her this was not appropriate and downright confusing. After running in circles and pulling on each other's hair for some time, we hit upon a compromise. The girl would be called Anna Bella Eema. The process was alphabetical. And Anna Bella Cello was too absurd. And so Anna Bella Eema it was.

Three into one trailer equals one size too small. They are rattling at the walls, shaking the very glass from the panes. I try and pull them in to story time. I open *Call of the Wild*, an old favourite of mine, a childhood edition with hand-painted pictures. I hold up the book, and turn to page one –

Two Mother, can't you see I'm too old for that book? Mother, we want to go out.

One There is more than one way to go out, Annabella.

Outside is a state of mind. And they are both at the window, hands clasped, eyes wild. They turn circles on the threshhold. They spin out the door.

It is a welcome camaraderie. Gives me time for my work.

These are the things Anna Bella and Anna Bella Eema do while I'm inside licking stamps.

Count simultaneously.

Two and Three begin to whisper-count as One speaks.

Dig deep holes in the ground.

Kiss behind the trailer home: Hands, Eyelids, Lips.

Capture crickets to dress like little girls.

Drain the silver liquid from the moon so they can sip it all by themselves.

Make strawberry pancakes.

Read Thoreau.

Jump up and down until the earth quakes beneath my trailer home and the dust rises in great, thick clouds.

Laugh.

Two laughs for a moment while Three keeps counting.

Climb trees.

Laugh.

Three laughs while Two keeps counting.

Stand on their heads.

Three and Two laugh together, now.

Give each other mud-puddle baths.

Laugh.

Pray.

Laugh.

Lace each other's boots.

Laugh.

Three and Two finish laughing.

One I was visited by a vampire once. He crawled out from beneath my trailer home, held his head in his hands, and he wept. 'My mother warned me the day I was born. That I would try and try and try, but never belong to the world. Now, after years of craving, I see she was right. Remember me.' He took off his cape, turned into a bat, and flew away.

She produces a cape.

This is the cape.

One puts the cape on.

Now it is the three of us on the pull-out couch. Anna Bella lies on my right side and Anna Bella Eema on my

20

left. It's the only way we can all sleep. Anna Bella curls up beneath one of my arms and Anna Bella Eema beneath the other. They make sweet eyes at each other for a while, but eventually, they are quiet.

Two and Three breathe.

Their breathing makes me think about the ocean. I went there once, when I was a little girl. It was a dark night. I flew there on the back of a swan. The moon was out. The ocean was dark with white waves surfacing like the baby teeth of little girls. The swan says, 'This is the ocean. You are on the bottom.' I laugh and bury my face in her feathers. 'That is not me,' I say. 'Those are other little girls.' The moon speaks: 'You are on the bottom. And the water is so heavy you cannot move.' I wave my arms: 'Look at me! I am moving!' And the swan says: 'Are you really moving?' And the moon says: 'Are you really moving?' And I realise that I am not. Really moving. I can feel the water pressing down. Immobilising me. I am at the bottom of the ocean. It is dark and quiet and the swan is drowned beside me. The water presses down and I feel a tentacle slide around my ankle. I am on the bottom of the ocean.

I am on the pull-out couch. Anna Bella and Anna Bella Eema have wrapped themselves around me in their sleep. They cling to me and breathe.

I have never been to the ocean.

Two bangs and clangs on a cookie sheet with a spoon.

Two My name is Annabella and these are my teeth.

She bares her teeth.

This is what happens when you are born from your mother when she is only fifteen years old. There was still so much calcium pulsing through her! I am hungry for it even in the womb. I drain it from her long before I even know what a tit looks like.

This is what my mom is like when I speak to her:
Mom, can I watch TV?

All three women make a catatonic face.

Mom, can I make some chocolate pudding?

All three women make a catatonic face.

Mom, can I please go on a killing spree?

All three women make a catatonic face.

I have so much freedom it gets boring. I don't even have any friends to brag to.

We have been living in this trailer park for as long as I can remember. I suppose I was born here.

A lot has changed since then. As you can see, we are the only trailer left in this trailer park. But there used to be more.

One takes out a small tape recorder and presses play: sounds of a child's trailer park play-world.

Victor lived one home over with his mom Val. Victor was one year younger than me and a fucking horny bastard. Nine years old and all he ever begged for was blow-jobs. I told him I'd give him one if he'd kiss me with his mouth open like they did on soap operas. He thought that was way too gross, so we were both out of luck. Across the dirt from us was Chris and Curtis Crystal and their mom Charlene. Charlene had inherited a luxury trailer from her grandmother and one whole room was filled up by this big white circle-bed. A bed in the shape of a circle! When Charlene would leave on her boyfriend's motorcycle, Chris, Curtis and I would spend hours and hours playing space station or ferry boat or Las Vegas Show Girls on Parade. I have never seen a Las Vegas showgirl, but Curtis has and he showed us how to put on the fishnet stockings he stole from Dollar General and the feathers he gutted from his pillow. There was also Joanie and Forrest and their mom Brenda-who-cried-all-the-time. And Misha, Alexis and their mom Masha who came to our trailer park all the way from Russia. Everyone was outside all the time. Or piling into our home for story time with Mom. Or daring each other to kick the plywood nailed to our trailer home to see what would come running out.

Edge of town, edge of forest, edge of cell signal, spotty wi-fi, spotty mailman, spotty electricity, blame it on the trees, downing power lines, gather round the camp fire Misha! Curtis! Marshmallows! Shoo racoons shoo! These are for humans!

One and Two laugh with delight.

It was a fun life. And then they were gone.

Silence.

Something is coming. It's either the interstate or the end of the world.

On the day I made my little girl out of mud, I was really really really really really really really bored. I had been trying to get my mother's attention all morning:
MOTHER, WE ARE THE ONLY ONES LEFT.

One licks a stamp.

MOTHER, THIS LETTER SAYS WE GOTTA LEAVE.

One licks a stamp.

MOTHER, I AM GOING TO BREAK THIS GLASS.

One holds up the broken glass. Then licks a stamp.

I am only ten years old but she fills me with the rage of a powerless middle-aged man. She will not act and I want to destroy the world. She will not act and I want to destroy people, methodically, in the way that one man can methodically destroy the self-esteem of an entire race. She makes me very very very very very very very very mad.

23

I cannot live without her. I pray inside every time the social worker comes to visit.

One recites the following over and over, low, as Two talks to the social worker.

One
For my sake and for hers
I beseech you Lord
Save us, for we are perishing.

Three Well well well, you have many books.

Two Yes, those are my mother's books. She reads to me every day.

Three Well I see you have a copy of *Catcher in the Rye*. That is an old favourite of mine.

Two Yes, it is very good, I like the characters very much.

Three Wasn't that book banned for a time, in most elementary schools?

Two What a stupid book. I don't like the characters very much.

Three This home is very clean.

Two (*aside, to audience*) Mother says something about ribs catching on fire in the oven. Please, Mother, don't be obscure! William Faulkner can be obscure, but NOT YOU!

Three So, Annabella, how have you been feeling lately?

Pause. One and Three provide the music for Two's aria.

Two (*sings*)
The blue iris,
sign of the fool-crow
sign of the ever-hopeful crow

is fading from my eye
I am growing fierce as time itself
I am growing wild and all-knowing
like a hornèd owl I am near you
even when you don't want me near you

I am only ten years old
this is the burden I carry
to be wise as the sky itself
and powerless as a crow at night

I carry all this danger
I carry all this revolution
but I am only ten years old
I cannot harness anything
These things I carry carry me

I am only ten years old
I make the fox run
And the wolf cry
What's a girl to do with this kind of knowledge
What's a girl to do with this kind of pain
I make the fox run
And the wolf cry.

Three (*speaks*) Anna Bella?

Two (*sings*)
 I'm feeling very tired now.

We always get out from under the social worker's thumb
by the skin of our teeth.

 She bares her teeth.

Now Misha and Masha's trailer is quiet and dark. Cock-
eyed and crooked, fallen off one of its blocks. A fox runs
in circles where Val's trailer used to be. She would come
over mornings, bathrobe and red platform shoes, petting
Mama's hair.

Two *and* **Three** Stay with us, gorgeous, no need to burrow down so deep. Ireeeeene? Stay out here with us.

Two If Val was gone, she'd send Charlene. Someone always keeping watch. And then Val is before me crying, suitcases piled outside our door.

Two and Three You're going to be OK, you're a big girl, right sweetie?

Two Scrambling and cursing, taxis and pickups and station wagons with mountains of possessions tied to the top – whoosh!
     On the day I made my little girl out of mud I was aching to make a mess. Momma wasn't moving, and there was EXTRA NOTHING TO DO! So I threw a book and a glass and went outside to pout. But I didn't feel like pouting so I started kicking the dirt. And then I decided get on her nerves since she was getting on mine, so I started singing her that song she hates. A song by the gentleman they call Oliver who-shot-the-la-la Morgan.

> Who shot the La La
> I don't know
> Who shot the La La
> I don't know
> Who shot the La La
> I don't know
> I think it was a 44.

Dumb enough to haunt you for weeks! In order to really get under her skin I decided to get as muddy as humanly possible. Spit. Sweat. Piss. Ouch, a little blood. Tears. Got enough liquid in me to make a fine mud puddle. See me mix it up. See me stick my ass in it. See me rubbing it into my belly button. See me lay down flat. Build a little hill on the ground in front of me. See me give that hill eyes. See me give that hill a mouth. See me sing to the hill.

Who shot the La La
I don't know
Who shot the La La
I don't know –

See me see the hill move. See me touch the hill on the forehead. See me see the hill's mouth move. See me put my finger inside the hill's mouth, and feel a stone. See me pull the stone out of the hill's mouth. See it come to life.

Three coughs violently, coughing up three stones.

Um. Hi.

Three smiles directly at Two.

MOOOOOOOOOOOOOM!

Tumbling thoughts as Anna Bella runs to her mom.

Man has nothing that animals have not at least a vestige of, the animals have nothing that man does not in some degree share. We are creatures of habit, and our habits lie in appetites formed a long long long long long long long time before we were born. The earth spins, our hearts rise into our throats, we desire so much it exceeds our skin. My mother's skin is very thin. But her bones are thick. Her bones are not human: They are the bones of a werewolf, trapped beneath woman-skin. She sits still to keep them from howling. But she has no idea what I can hear.

One howls a distant howl.

It doesn't take us long to realise that Anna Bella Eema can't speak. Or won't speak.
She will open her mouth.

Three does so.

She will stick out her tongue.

Three does so.

She will lick her chops.

Three does so.

She will smile.

Three does so.

But she will not form words. In spite of her silence, I take to her immediately. She is our orphan. She has all the time in the world. Anna Bella Eema takes me to many, many places. Places my mother wouldn't dare go. And when she says go, we really GO.

A rhythmic travelogue, backed up by Three and One.

To the grocery store to buy five jars of pickles with our pennies which we eat native style right there in the parking lot.

To a crack in the pavement which has taken on the shape of an evil eye.

To the bulldozers behind the trailer, where the vampires live.

Pause in rhythm-making.

Did you know vampires live on construction sites? We go there just after the whistle blows and watch them emerge. The vampires are a sorry lot in these parts. They lope about on cranes, lamenting the death of everything. 'Eck! Not even a tree left to piss behind! Even the babies die young! Look around at all this concrete and yellow paint. There is nothing to eat here – no way to make more. Eck! It is all beginning to cease!'

Rhythm-making starts again.

To the remote clearing in the woods where the police tape still clings to the trees. where she teaches me a short self-defence class. Hi ya!

To the inside of my mother's tear duct. (Echo. Echo. Echo.)

To a place I call the 'Valley of Silverspot' which is very very wet and very very elusive and very very slippery and intense.

To the crawl space beneath the trailer home.

Rhythm-making stops: we will spend some time here.

It was a long long long time before she could get me to crawl under there with her. She would take me to the entrance spot and pull away the plywood, and this cool air would come out and stream up my nostrils and wrap itself around my skull. Whoo! I knew I couldn't go in there until I could smell that air and not be light-headed. And then one day I breathed in and did not sway or swoon. Anna Bella Eema stands holding the plywood covering. Smiling and motioning for me to go in like this.

She shows us how Anna Bella Eema motioned.

I scratch my belly like this.

She shows us how she scratches her belly.

I gather my courage like this.

She does a courage-gathering motion.

And I go inside the cold and the dark.

One On the day my little girl made a girl I found myself very very very very very very lonely. I am not usually a lonely woman. I have my books and my stamps and my hawk's eye unceasing. My girl leaves me every day, after her schooling, to go play jacks or climb a tree. It shouldn't make any difference that today she leaves with another girl with her.

Her start in life was a good mother, a reliable instinct and more than a germ of reason. It was her creative instinct, inherited from me, that allowed my little girl to make a girl. I noticed right away that little mud girl had my eyes. Still my head fills with sounds of warning:

One and Two sing the sounds of warning. Three sings a 'translation'.

One, Two	Three
Kwit Kwit	Fly Fly
Rrrrrrrrr	Danger
K-reet	Come
Help Help	Help Help
Rrrrrrrrr	Danger
Crrrraaaaaw	I love you
Ca ca ca ca Caw	Scatter for your lives
That is Man Scent	That is Man Scent
Rrrrrrrrr	Danger

One I start to lick stamps. I feel pressure on my back. I hear the sound of construction, growing closer. I pick up the paper the manager shoved into my hands.

Interstate On Ramp.

Cell Phone Tower.

I feel pressure on my chest. I lick stamps faster. I hear Anna Bella and Anna Bella Eema playing outside.

Two When Thoreau says 'Let us improve our opportunities, before the evil days come,' he must refer to the approaching onslaught of capitalism, I mean really –

Three gives her a look: she is sceptical of Two's interpretation.

I'm certain of it. Now teach me that spell that makes the crickets dance.

Three sings the following spell. She sounds a little like a theremin. It goes on beneath One's next speech.

Three
EEEE-LEEEE
AAAA-BAAA
BAAA-AAAA
LAAA-EEEEE

NAAA-NAAA
BAAA-BAAA
EEEM-MAAA

One The pressure on my chest increases. I try to keep licking stamps. It is difficult. To distract myself, I picture my little girl and me as grey wolves. I am the mother wolf and she is the cub. She follows my every move. I can feel her warm, silky cub-fur brush against mine. If I take a step, she takes a step. If I sleep, she sleeps. This is good, I think, as she nestles into my fur, this is the way of the wild. And then one day while napping, we are attacked by a pack of hyenas. I leap away and so she . . . and so she . . . she is second. She does not make it. Even though I taught her everything I know. She does not make it. She is wide open. All that is left are her ribs and her teeth.

Three's cricket spell has turned into a moan/howl. One joins in. The howling goes on and then stops.

And then I am standing on my stamp-licking table. Anna Bella Eema is the hyena. My teeth hurt. The envelopes are on the floor. I smell bad. Anna Bella Eema is the hyena. The stamps are sticky, all over my hands.

Through the kitchen window I see my little girl rub her belly like this.

One and Two rub their bellies.

I see her move her arms like this.

One and Two gather their courage.

Then I hear something happening underneath the house.

Two I had never been under there before. I went in and the temperature dropped ten degrees and I began to sweat. Light streamed in from behind me where Anna Bella Eema stood, still holding the plywood open. Water dripped down from the corner of the home where the

31

sink stood. I could see some old cigarette packages. And
the ball I lost last summer. And a single earthworm
crawling like a drunkard through the dust. Hmm. Not
much here at all, I thought.

And then Anna Bella Eema shuts the plywood door.

(*Sings.*)

Her hands are on me.
She has so many hands!
She can touch all of me at once.
It is dark with light streaming in through the cracks
But I cannot see all of her.
She is huge, now.
She takes up the whole underneath
She is underneath me.
I dig my toes into her skin
She is above me.
I dig my hands into her now-enormous tits.
Everywhere I put my hand
I feel her hand. Or her foot. Or her ribs. Or her mouth.
Her mouths. She has many mouths.
One of her mouths is as curious as a cat.
It is on my eyes. On my neck. On my ribs and hips.
One of her mouths is bold as a bear.
Tongue in my mouth, lips in my throat, teeth in my
    heart.
This mouth finds its way inside without being nice.
One of her mouths she uses to speak.
Underneath the trailer home.
This is where her words live.

One, Two *and* **Three** Annabella, Annabella, Annabella,
this is your creation speaking. This is what it means to be
an individual, Annabella. This is what it means to be free:
To be free is to be origin. To be origin is to be a slayer of
images. To be a slayer of images is to be more than
another set of bones wandering across the earth. To be

more than another set of bones wandering across the earth is to realise that you are just another set of bones wandering across the earth. To be just another set of bones wandering across the earth is to be human. To be human is to be alive. To be alive is to have the capacity to create something outside of yourself. To have the capacity to create something outside of yourself is to be magic. To be magic is to be of the earth. To be of the earth is to be of the stars. To be of the stars is to be simultaneously ancient and eternal. To be simultaneously ancient and eternal is to be origin. To be origin is to be free.

Two She is all around me. She is everywhere I put my hand. One of her mouths pulls my chest out of my chest. One of her mouths gnaws at my hips. A shock, a rush, up my legs: Am I, am I – headache into belly – a mouth shapes my bones? Eema Bella Am I Am I –

I am rolling over her skin. I am clawing at the plywood covering. I am in the back yard.

I am out of breath.

Anna Bella Eema peers out from underneath the trailer home: two bright eyes and a smile curling upward, I look down at myself and see – ah! – the beginnings of breasts.

And my hips feel wobbly in their sockets. And on the ground, between my feet. One. Two. Three round drops of blood.

Through the dust and the darkness, she looks at me and grins. An owl hoots, clouds bloom open. I feel like I am ninety years old. And then there is a total eclipse of the sun, and the ground lifts up to catch my withered head.

Two faints to the ground and is very, very still.

One I am pulling myself together and trying to lick stamps again. The table is clean and I return to my routine. My routine is my routine. This new girl cannot mean the end of everything I call my own.

33

I am licking stamps. It is still difficult. The new girl
comes in and lays her head down on my lap like a puppy
dog. I jiggle my legs like this to try and get her off. She
doesn't budge. I ask her:

Anna Bella Eema. Move.

She will not budge.

Anna Bella Eema. Move.

Nothing.

Anna Bella Eema. What do you want?

She pops up, and goes to the door. She motions for me
to come out, like this.

*One demonstrates the motion that Anna Bella Eema
made.*

I put my hands on my hips like this.

She demonstrates how she put her hands on her hips.

Anna Bella Eema, you know I don't go outside. Where is
Anna Bella?

And she gets this look in her eye that says 'Something
has happened.' My little girl. Something has happened to
my own little girl. I am off the floor, flying over the table
through the door. I soar over the top of the trailer home,
my housecoat billowing in the wind. I land beside her in
the back yard. She is on the ground, out cold. There are
three spots of blood by her feet, and a trail of blood
down her leg. WHAT HAVE YOU DONE TO MY GIRL
WHAT HAVE YOU DONE!

*Three looks shocked, hurt. She begins to cry: she's
done nothing wrong.*

Is this my little girl? You are so big. I cannot fold you
into my hand, I cannot gather you into the pocket of my
cheek. I look at you and see you increasing. You will
surpass me and leave me behind like an apple core or a
too-small shoe. Are you my little girl?

A bulldozer crouches at the edge of the forest, its jaws hungry for us. Anna Bella Eema helps me pull her on to my back. Then it's back up over the trailer house, through the door and straight to the pull-out couch. She is still bleeding. Only ten years old. Starting young, like her mother. I curse myself for being her mother. I want to set her free. I want to protect her. I want her to run wild. I want her to stay right here with me. I wash her. I make her a diaper out of old sheets. She sleeps like the child that she is as I wrap it around her, pinning it with a single pin between her hips.

I hear her breathing. And the sound of construction. Outside. Getting closer.

I cannot lick any more stamps today.

Outside. Getting closer.

I sit at the table. Anna Bella Eema fixes me a drink with some leftover liquor and cough syrup scrounged from the cabinets. She places it before me and sits across the table. We are silent for a long time while I drink.

One drinks.

[We are silent but she is looking at me. Her look says: 'What will you do now? The Buldozers are gnawing at your front door. How will you protect her now?'

She keeps looking and looking, so finally I speak.

She sings.

I would rip the pipes out of their throats
If I had the arched teeth of a jaguar
I would feed on their hearts in the road that they laid
I would plunge my claws into the base of their skulls
If these two hands were four paws

I would fix my eye on the foreman's shoulder
If I had the hooked craw of a hawk
I would pluck the light from his sleeping eye
I would perch on the mount of his chest
If this mouth were a beak black and pointed

35

I can feel my spine lengthening
And my skin growing coarse
One hair two hair three hair four
Anima animal enemy mine

We will fix our night eyes on their sleeping children
When we have the spry feet of wolves
We will feed on the dreams that hide in the
tender flesh behind their ears, beneath their tongues
deep in the arch of their foot.
And we will leave them to rot on their cold concrete
As we make our escape
So fast and close to the ground we laugh and howl
Our sharp teeth dripping –

*Three stomps loud on the floor, three times. The song
stops.*]

*Three stomps three more times, louder. One downs her
drink.*
    Three stomps four or five times, loud.

Somebody's at the door.

  *Three gives her a look like, 'What do you want me to
  do about it?'*

Anna Bella Eema ducks behind the pull-out couch.

  Three stomps three times, again.

Somebody's at the –

  *Three makes a creaking sound of the door opening.
  She speaks in a deep, low voice.*

Three Hello. Is anybody home?

One [The Monster] Frankenstein is at the door. He is
disguised as a police officer. His broad chest makes his
police shirt pop open. His badge is pinned through his
greenish skin, above his left nipple. The bolts in his neck

ooze a light green pus. His hands are enormous. One of
them unconsciously drifts to the frightening bulge in his
too tight pants, an erection so huge I get a sharp pain in
my lower back. He stands over me, his head bowed so he
can fit inside the trailer home.

Three Ma'am, I come to you as a representative of the
Department of Transportation, bringing crucial upgrades
for our future. Ma'am, its time to go. The project is
practically upon your home. To be honest I am surprised
to find you here, ma'am, I'm surprised at you. Have
you not received this red card with information relocation
assistance? Have you not activated the online Relocation
Assistance Vouchers for Foodland, SuperFixIt, Drug
Emporium, PetWorld, Office World, Pools Incorporated
plus $500 directly deposited into your bank? Ma'am, do
you have a bank account? I myself took advantage of
these benefits, ma'am, and I can tell you it makes for a
sweet life. Ma'am, did you receive this red card in the
mail? Ma'am? Ma'am?

One I got the card in the mail.

Three Can you read it, ma'am? Ma'am?

One I read. I know how you have spied on me.

Three Ma'am, have you been drinking? Ma'am, the
Department of Transportation wants you to consider this
your last warning before you are forcibly removed, so
please, ma'am, I am asking you politely to –
    Whoo now what's this? Ma'am, is this your daughter
lying asleep here on this pull-out couch?

One That's my daughter.

Three And ma'am, can you tell me how she got that
scrape on her right shoulder and that bruise on her left?

One I think she fell.

Three You think she fell?

One I think she was underneath the trailer home.

Three Ma'am, did she fall or was she underneath the house. Ma'am? Fall or underneath?

Three tries to wake up Two, who is still passed out on the floor.

Wake up, little lady. How'd you get so scratched up? You can tell me, it's OK. Wake up, little lady. It's me, Mister Policeman. Wake up – why won't she wake up?

One She's tired.

Three *Really* tired apparently.

One She's got her female problems right now.

Three Oh well now, I don't know anything about that.

Silence.

One I know how you have spied on me.

Three Ma'am, have you been drinking?

Silence.

This is your last warning. Get out, or we'll get you out.

One He pushes the door open with one finger and squeezes himself through. Outside he unfolds to full size. Scratches his eye. Straightens his badge. Tries to push down his erection, poor thing. It will not go down. Assumes police posture, chest out, eyes glazed. And strides away.

I know how he has spied on me. When I was a little girl, these parts were so alive even Frankenstein lived nearby. He lived in the woods but he never came out because he knew people would fear him. But he would come very close so he could watch us play: kick the can. Hopscotch. Tackle the man with the ball. Freeze tag.

I was always the only one who saw him.

One reminds us of her eye.

The mud girl sits across from me with that look in her
eye.

There are many ways to go out, I say. Outside is a
state of mind.

She crawls over me and curls into the bend of my girl's
knee. Anna Bella Eema is not the hyena. But Anna Bella
Eema is not mine. She belongs to the grown creature my
girl is becoming, a creature all her own. Each hour of
each day I wipe my girl's brow with a damp wet cloth.
Each hour of the five days I rub her tiny little girl feet.

This went on for five days straight.

On the evening of the fifth day [the Monster]
Frankenstein returned. He was not in uniform. He
lowered his lips to the crack in the window over the sink,
and spoke.

Three OK, here are the things I wanted to say but did
not say because I am such a small and inarticulate
monster. I know you saw me seeing you all these years.
I know this is your home, the place you fit into. I have
been in your position. I mean, your psychological
position. I mean, I have never lived in a trailer home. I
came out of nowhere and took to the forest, where I lived
on berries and the meat of small animals. I lived in the
forest. When it rained I got wet. When it snowed I got
cold. It was my place to be. I have been in your position.
I too was filled with rage when they came to me in their
suits and asked me to relocate. I scared the fuck out of
them with my cry –

Three lets out a bone-chilling cry.

And with my enormous hands and of course with my
enormous genitals. That was especially scary for a lot of

39

the guys. But they kept coming back. They started sending old ladies. Old ladies who had seen it all. Unflappable grandmothers that laughed at my cry and didn't even blink at the cock. And they convinced me. This place is not the only place. You don't always have to stand your ground. Sometimes, you just take the vouchers. I took the vouchers and a job, too. It makes for a sweet life, I assure you.

I know you have the eye of a hawk and the heart of a monster.

One looks shocked: how does he know of her monster heart?

A benevolent monster like me. I know you feel the earth's anima pulsing up through the trees and out into the electric sky. You sense the pull of the supernatural with such animal clarity that to go outside would mean to relinquish your earthly shape, become part of the ravenous wild.

But you are wrong. You are a woman. You have the body of a woman. You can live in their world if you so choose.

I am never coming back here. I've been asked to be assigned to a different precinct. Coming back here makes me sad.

Irene, choose the sweet life. Because also you are sweet.

Three sings.

Your bones are cold
And your teeth are chattering
And your toes are frozen
And your spine's a-shivering
And wind is blowing sharp
Through your jaw.
And your palms are chilly
And there's frost on the nape of your neck

And the icicles drip from the back of your throat
And your skull's gone cold.

All I want
Is to take you in
Wrap you in the warm blanket
I carry here in the cavern of my heart.

*All at once Two snaps awake: a huge gasp. She leaps
on to her chair.*

Two I am asleep for five whole days. During these five
days I went on an adventure. To my mother inside the
trailer home, it appeared as though I was sound asleep
in my bed. The only way I can explain what happened
is to say that Anna Bella Eema arranged it so I could take
a trip to a very different world. But at the same time she
allowed me to sleep soundly, here, on the pull-out couch!
Here is what happened.

*One and Three begin to create the soundscape of
Two's dreamworld.*

Wait.

One and Three stop.

I want to tell you that this adventure took five days. To
you, it will seem like a few short minutes. Just imagine
everything I tell you as taking longer, and being way
more intense. OK.

One and Three begin again.

Anna Bella Eema peers out from underneath the trailer
home: two bright eyes and a set of white teeth smiling.
I feel like I am ninety years old. And then there is a total
eclipse of the sun and I feel myself begin to faint.
    And then I am in the middle of green. A bright green
hill among many hills. A lemon yellow sun. A flock of

fire-engine-red birds, over a pond of sky-blue water.
Everything crisp and alive, like the pictures in my
mother's favourite wild-life books.

And I was inside the book!

I stand on the hill and take in my surroundings. I feel
something wriggling round my ankles, and I look down
to see: a mysterious racoon with its grubby racoon paws
on my knees –

Two screams.

One Anna Bella –

Two Said the racoon –

One My name is Dirty Lou, and I am your guide. We've
been expecting you, of course. Show me your teeth.

Two bares her teeth. One is unimpressed.

One Right. Come with me.

Two Balancing on his hind legs, he unfolds a blue cap
from the palm of his hand, and places it on his head.
He scratches the grey fur on his belly, then stomps one
foot, then the other foot, and a second creature burrows
forth, coughing off the dirt. A hyena. With two bright
eyes and a smile curling upward.

Three smiles.

One Alright, then. Follow us.

Two And he is off down the hill, waddling upright on
two racoon feet –

One Stay close –

Two He said –

One You'll never make it with those teeth.

Two Dirty Lou took me on a very long journey, and it was hard to keep up. The hyena tracked us the whole time. He took me down the hill, across the fields, into the woods, out of the woods, through the pasture, over a bridge, into a canyon, up the river, through a tiny tunnel, into the gulf, out of the gulf, across the desert, around a dormant volcano and an ancient, dry seabed, until we arrive at a hilltop that looked suspiciously like the hilltop where we had started.

And I am very, very tired.

One You look very, very tired.

Two He stretches out against the trunk of an old oak tree.

One Come now. Lie down here on my soft racoon lap.

Two And I did. He gazes out into the distance, with my head on his lap. The hyena curls into the bend of my knees.

She speaks to Dirty Lou.

Why are we going in circles?

One To keep you in one place, of course.

Two But I want to move. I want to see things.

One Like this?

Two Dirty Lou waves his paw and I go dizzy. The world splits static, images flash. Lips, Eyelashes, Bottles of Pretty, Ageless Necklines, YES! Positivity Stamped on a Coffee Mug, Arched Backs and Perfect Homes, Perfect Smiles, Swish! Smiles –

One It's too much to fight, Anna Bella. Those milk-fed little miracles are going to waste.

Two What?

One Shhh. Such a gentle little girl. Open your mouth.

Two And I did.
   And he reaches his paw down, down, down. As his own mouth opens I see I see I see he HAS NO TEETH.

One Perfect. So white and sharp. Just what I've been looking –

Two And in an instant I BITE his grubby paw as HARD AS I CAN! I feel it snap!

One Ow!

Two (*holding up a claw*) This is the claw I snapped from the paw of Dirty Lou, the racoon.

One The nerve of you! You'll never make it! Don't you understand?

Two His head whips back and forth, and the hyena jumps to her feet. She is crying into the sky, calling something out of the clouds, mouth opening wider and wider –

One Watch yourself, girl. This is real life. Real life.

Two And WHOOSH! I am nabbed at the nape of the neck and taken up up up into the sky. Pastures, waters, a picture-perfect barn, a precision cut-out of a mountain on the horizon. Up, up, up through the branches of an evergreen trees. Scratches and cuts on my face and on my arms. And then dropped! I am dropped!
   Right into a giant nest. In the crook of the branch of the same tree. And I see that I have been carried there by an owl. She is fat with a flat face and a green shawl around her shoulders. Shoulders broad, eyes closed.

One We've got to get out of here! Racoons can swim! Grab the oars. *Now!*

Two Grab the what?

One Grab the oars and *row*.

Two And I did. I grab two wooden oars and with my head down and my feet braced I row and row and row. I feel my shoulders growing older and my hands growing tough. But still I row and row and –

One Annabella. You can rest now. We've come a long, long way.

Two And I raise my eyes and see: we are in a tiny boat. In the middle of a vast sea!

One You are safe in this nest. My name is Bertha –

Two Hi, Bertha.

One And this is my kitty.

Two A sleek, grey cat creeps up to perch on Bertha's shoulder, licking its paws. A cat on an owl's shoulder. A cat with a hyena smile. It is smiling at me.

One So, Anna Bella. Can you see the sea?

Two Yes!

One All around you? For miles and miles?

Two Yes. A liquid surface all around me.

One I knew you the had the eyes for it. There aren't many people who truly know how to see. Your mother, for example, has never seen the ocean.

Two My mother is a woman who is afraid to leave her trailer home.

One And you?

Two I am not a woman who is afraid to leave her trailer home.

One Exactly. But have *you* seen the ocean?

Two I am only ten years old.

One Exactly. That's exactly what she said when she was your age.

Two Bertha begins to hum.

One begins to hum.

The cat begins to purr.

Three begins to purr in 'harmony' with the owl's hum.

Bertha wipes my brow with a damp cloth. So nice. I am in a tiny boat in the centre of the sea. And the owl with the cat by her side is singing to me.

One (*sings*)
    Sail the sea
    Holy See
    ABC
    You can see

    See the sea
    Not the tree
    You can see
    Easily

    You will see the ocean
    You will be stronger
    You will know the ground beneath your feet
    You will kill what you have to kill

    Sail the ——
    Holy——
    A B ——
    You can ——

    You will see
    You will be
    You will know
    You will kill

    You will see
    You will kill.

One and Three continue to hum and purr.

One presses the palm of her hand to her wrist, as though she is wiping Anna Bella's forehead with a damp cloth.

One You're a lucky girl, Annabella. You've seen everything you need to see. You don't need those eyes. Now open them wide . . .

Two And I did. And for the first time I see I see that Bertha is blind! She *snaps* at my right eye, I dodge. She *snaps* at my left eye, I dodge again. I scramble to the edge of the boat. I see – trees? We haven't gone anywhere at all.

(*To Bertha.*) We haven't gone anywhere at all!

One Exactly. Now come here!

Two She *snaps* again and I grab hold of a feather in between *her* eyes. The cat *screeches*. The feather *pops*.

One Ow! Now is that any way to treat your mother? Hmmm?

Two This is the feather I plucked from the eye of Bertha the owl.

Two shows us the feather.

Three Psst. Psst. Psst.

Two I look down, down, down and I see a fox at the base of the tree. It is tiny and wears a bright red scarf.

One takes off shawl and glasses and dons a red pilot's scarf.

Three Foxes can't climb trees! You must leap. Leap!

Two And I did. I leap down, down, down, past the branches and the bark and beetles and the leaves, and land on the ground on my own two feet.

The fox looks deep into my eyes.

47

During the next section, Three speaks the lines of the fox, but One plays the fox. It is as though the fox is speaking to Anna Bella telepathically, without opening its mouth.

Two What are you doing?

Three I am trying to glimpse your little bird soul that is flying around inside the cage of your chest.

Two Why?

Three So it can fly away.

Two Do you want me to die?

Three I want you to live.

Two Can you see it? Can you see my little bird soul?

The fox stares into Annabella's soul.

And you will never believe what happened next. As the fox stared into me, a little blue bird began to materialise, slowly, on top of the fox's head. First its little bird feet came into focus, then the outline of its little bird body, then its blue colour, then beak, then eyes. A bird perched on a fox's head. And I swear I am not lying when I say that bird was smiling.

Three Let's go.

Two (*to the audience*) I want to make it clear to you that the fox spoke to me without using his voice. Somehow it spoke without speaking.

Three Let's go!

Two Wait. Show me your teeth.

One bares her teeth.

Perfect. And your eyes.

One blinks three times, or opens her eyes wide.

Nice work.

The fox took me on another long journey, and the bluebird fluttered with us the whole time. We went over the river, into the eye of the hawk, out of the eye of the hawk, up the wriggling mound, into the lake of the tongues, out of the lake of the tongues across the dried and brittle bones until we arrive at a clearing on the edge of a lush, green forest. The fox takes off my shoes and begins rubbing the journey out of my weary, tired feet.

Three Look how strong they've become.

Two What are we going to do now?

Three I am going to teach you how to kill.

Two The fox leads me behind the bushes. We peer through the branches together.

Three Every kind of animal has some great strength or it could not live, and some great weakness or others could not live. The squirrel's weakness, for example, is foolish curiosity, the fox's that it can't climb a tree. The training of an animal must be shaped to understand the weakness of the creatures that might harm it.

Two I watch the fox watch the tall grass outside the bush. Soon, the grass begins to tremble as though tiny fingers were pulling it from ground level. The fox rises up, just high enough to spring. It stays perfectly still, and then *leaps* from the bush and lands paws first on a pile of dead grass. And now it is chewing happily on a small, plump mouse.

The fox comes back to the bush, licking all traces of blood from its lips.

Three We start with the mouse, and its obvious weakness: mice are small. The things to remember: only hunt mice on calm days, for then you see the shaking of the grass. *See* with your whole body: eyes are important, but your instinct will save you. And finally, *do not hesitate* to dig in with your teeth. Fingers are clumsy. Teeth are sharp and strong.

Two I perch behind the bush with the fox, waiting for the grass to shiver. It moves, and I almost jump.

Three You cannot *almost* jump. That is exactly what they want you to do. When you move, *move*.

Two I wait again. The grass begins to shiver but the time was not yet right. I am concentrating as hard as I can.

Three She is concentrating as hard as she can. It is a beautiful sight to see. She exists in this moment for herself and her prey. And then she leaps.

Two I leap.

Three Her hands flatten the trembling grass.

Two I can feel a tiny life moving underneath. I do not hesitate.

Three She does not hesitate. She grinds her pearly little milk-teeth into the mouse with a rush of inborn savageness that must have surprised even herself.

Two The mouse is in my mouth. I can feel its life going away as I chew. I can feel it cease to exist.

Three It is bloodier than she imagined. Blood drips from the corners of her mouth.

Two The fox looks at me and I know that it is proud.

Three I teach her to lick all traces of blood from her lips.

One and Two lick their lips.

Two That mouse was so small. Such a small thing to kill.

Three Oh dear, there will be much bigger things. The

world will come for you, try to keep you in your place. But you are ready. This is real life.

Two And the fox smiles and tosses its head, side to side, and its head tosses and swirls into a blaze of orange as the blue bird materialises again, a brilliant blue flutter against the orange blaze and I feel the frothy foam waves nipping at the back of my heels and then I woke up.

One On the day my little girl finally woke up, she had a bright red scarf in her hand.

One gives the red scarf to Two.

Two This is the scarf.
    I woke up into this world and found it all too real. The trailer home smelled bad. My mother is usually a good housekeeper, but the the trash was overflowing and there were dishes in the sink and empty soda cans and banana peels on the floor. Mom's stamp-licking table is piled high with stuff, none of which is stamps. Yarn. Magazines. Half-eaten candy bars. Cold cream with the cap off. A pot of half-eaten ravioli with a hair brush in it.
    And she was nervous.

One I was nervous. About your condition, of course, but also because you are the one who usually goes out. I cannot go out. So no one goes out. Well, Anna Bella Eema snuck out once, but they didn't see her.

Two Who didn't see her?

One Don't worry, they didn't see her.

Two I look at Anna Bella Eema.

Three shrugs her shoulders.

I try to stand up. My legs are wobbly, and there is a sheet tied up around my crotch. Mother, what is this sheet?

One I kept you clean.

Two Mother, what is wrong with you? What's happening?

One You were asleep for five days. I kept rubbing your feet.

Two I go to the bathroom to clean myself up. The toilet is not flushing. I am finishing getting clean and then there is a face at the bathroom window.

Two screams a blood-curdling scream.

Three (*as a policeman*) Don't worry, little girl, I am here to help. I know you don't want to come outside.

Two Who are you?

Three I am with the State Department of Transportation.

Two Why are you outside my window?

Three We've been outside your trailer home for three days. Your mom won't let us in.

Pause. The situation begins to dawn on Two.

Two I leave the bathroom and go look out the living-room window.

One Don't open it!

Two I open it. I see a police car with two policemen in front of it, sitting in lawn chairs drinking coffee. I go to the other window.

One DON'T OPEN IT!

Two I see another police car with the light flashing but nobody inside. Behind it, a pack of construction workers are approaching in orange hard-hats.
Mother what is happening?

One You were asleep for five days.

Two Mother, what do those men want?

One They want to eat us alive.

Two Mother, please, please, not now. Wake up, Mother, wake up to this room. They told us this was going to happen, Mother, I told you this was going to happen.

One Don't worry, I will protect you. I have read many books.

Two Mother, I need to go out there.

Three makes danger sounds beneath the following lines of dialogue.

Three
Kwit Kwit
Rrrrrrrrr
K-reet
Scatter for your lives
Rrrrrrrrr
Crrrraaaaaw
Ca ca ca ca Caw
That is Man Scent
Rrrrrrrrrrrrrr.

Two I'll come right back.

One THEY WILL TAKE YOU! THEY WILL PUT US BEHIND BARS!

Two Mother, shhh. Please be quiet. They're going to think you're hurting me, Mother, please shhh.

Danger sounds fade.

One Listen to me. The life of a wild animal always has a tragic end. I will protect you.

Two Mother, I will come right back.

One But I'm frightened.

Two I take Anna Bella Eema's hand and guide her to my

mother's lap. I see my mother has grown quite thin. I can hear her bones whimper through her skin. Her eyes are tired. I put my hand on her jaw. It is very very very very very very cold.

Anna Bella Eema will be here with you. I will be right back.

Three (*sings*)
All I want
Is to take you in
Wrap you in the warm blanket
I carry here
In the cavern of my heart.

Two I opened the door and left my mother inside. It was bright out. I could barely see. There were four policemen, and I don't know how many construction workers. They hadn't seen any movement from our trailer home in three days. I'm amazed at how much the trailer park has changed. When they saw me, they all froze. There was nothing left. They had finally torn the sign down. And dug up all the hook-ups for electricity. And cut down almost every last tree. Now I can clearly see the approaching interstate and all the heavy equipment. It is all stopped in its tracks, waiting for my mother and me to move. For a moment, I feel quite proud.

Three Gentlemen, don't make a move. We don't want to scare her back inside.

Two Hi. Can you tell me what's going on? I was asleep.

Three So your momma tells us through the cracks in the windows. You mean to say you've been asleep for five days?

Two Yep.

Three Young lady, we've got to get you and your momma

out of there, unless you want to live your life under cold, hard concrete.

Two I know we have to move. But we've got to be careful. She's sensitive.

Three What do you mean, be careful?

Two For example. Is there any way we could pick up the trailer home, or put wheels on it and move it away with her inside?
   The pack of policemen and construction workers are completely silent.

Three You want us to do all that just to move that piece of crap?

Two I look back at our trailer home. And for the first time in my life, I really see it. The aluminum siding had turned nine shades of rust, with rust-holes patched up with duct-tape. Newspaper clings to the inside of the windows. A sign my mom made out of poster board –

One Keep Away Or Else.

Two – hangs crooked on a coathanger taped to the door. It's a disaster. Who would want to live in that trailer home?`
   (*To the policeman.*) Yes, you need to move it. Carefully. With her inside.
   The policemen and construction workers shift in their boots, grunting and scratching at their chests and crotches. Finally, the policeman I had been talking to leans over to me.

Three Now you are a sweet little girl. Come with Mr Policeman, and he will get you some juice.

Two He leans over and reaches his two arms beneath my

armpits, and tries to lift me off the ground. He should not do this. Because I immediately kick and scream, which makes my mother come outside.

Three, as Anna Bella Eema, bangs her hands on her table.

One We see him put his hands on my little girl and I feel my bones start to swell and my voice open up down my spine through the earth and up through the top of my head.

Three, as Anna Bella Eema, bangs her hands on her table.

Two We hear her before we see her, but it all happens incredibly fast.

Three, as Anna Bella Eema, bangs her hands on her table.

One The little mud-girl holds the door open wide, and I leap out to the centre of the yard on my back haunches, low to the ground and ready to spring.

Two Mr Policeman doesn't know what in the hell to do, so I see most of it. She is absolutely beautiful. Her eyes blaze and her jaw is set firm. They surround her.

One They surround me. My ribs expand and my hands grow large. The fur on the back of my arms stands up and my fangs press out against my upper lip. My lips are dripping and my shoulders arch up and out. They are all around me, now.

One of the hard hats makes a move. I let out a

One	**Two**	**Three**
(*Howls*)	Rrrrrrr	That daughter is MINE
	Ca ca ca Caw	Run for your life
	Rrrrrrr	MINE

Two The whole pack leaps back five feet. Then they

realise they are being scared by the crazy trailer-house lady. One of them strides forth.

One One of them strides forth, so I go for his neck.

One bares her teeth.

Two She lunges forth and bites a guy *bites a guy* in the shoulder. She is flailing her arms. They don't look thin any more. She bites the guy and he cries out like a little boy.

One A second cop comes at me with a long, wooden stake. He goes for my heart. but I am quick and he only pins my wrist to the ground.

Two She is pinned to the ground!

One He pokes and he pokes and he pokes, but the stick will not go through. I swipe at his chest and dig my fangs into his face.

Two And she is up! Her dress is torn and her hands are bleeding, but her eyes are sharp and her legs powerful and spry. She bounds to the corner of our trailer home. WATCH OUT, MOTHER, THEY ARE GOING AROUND BACK!
The policeman gets mad at me for yelling, so he puts me in the car, but I can still see, sort of.

One I can feel them behind the trailer home. I am concentrating very hard. Instincts are more accurate than eyes in this case.
I notice some blood on the top of one of my forelegs. I lick it off, and lick down my fur.

Two She crouches by the corner of the trailer home, filling her fists with rusty nails so they stick out like claws.

One My spine is alive and ready.

Two My mother is a wild mother. I hear her entire being growl.

One When I am sure they are coming around the corner, I leap at them, claws fully extended. I feel one go into an eye and one into a thigh. But one policeman has a gun, and he uses it.

Three makes the sound of a gunshot.

Two A gun goes off a gun goes off a gun goes off MOOOOOOOOOOOOOM.

One (*whispers*) The gun does not hit me, but I play like it did.

Two She is hit! Let me out! Let me out!

Two makes the sound of pounding.

One (*to her daughter*) Wait. I am coming.

Two stops pounding – she hears her mother.

I fling myself down and grab my leg and flap my arm over and over again on the ground like a wounded bird Mercy oh mercy! Help I am hit! Oh help! They send one cop for a stretcher, and the others hang back, curious. Water, oh please, just a little water! I look into the eye of one of the weak ones, and he immediately steps forth with his water bottle. He opens the cap and kneels down next to me, and I *swipe* at his face and *plunge my fangs* into his hand, and I am up and running towards the car where my daughter is held hostage. She is pressed against the window.

Two She breaks free from the pack.

One My muscles are firm. I am covered now with a thick, rough fur. I see Frankenstein spying from the woods. He is crying out, crying –

Three (*as Frankenstein*) Stop! Go back! Stop!

One The tears are streaming down his face, but I am unstoppable. I am bounding towards her.

Two I am pressed against the window and she is running towards me. She is gigantic Her face is changing shape. First a racoon, then an owl, then a fox, then a wolf coming towards me. She is graceful and unstoppable.

One I leap towards her.

Two She is coming towards me on all fours. She is in the air.

Three makes the sound of a gunshot.

One And they get me. I am stunned.

Two MOM!

Three It's just a stun-gun, little lady, don't be afraid.

One I hit the ground.

Two She hits the ground hard. She is so heavy, the whole earth quakes.

Two and Three make the sound of the earth rumbling.

One I lift my broad right paw into the air, but something is terribly wrong. Only fingers. Skinny grey fingers, wriggling in front of my face. And then the lights go out.

One slumps in her chair.

Two I squirm out of the car. She is curled in a ball on the ground. She is so tiny she could fit in the palm of my hand. Her skin has turned grey from never going out. Her eyes sink in. Her shoulder blades poke out at absurd angles. Most of her dress has been ripped off of her in the struggle. Her face is cut. Foam gathers in the corners of her mouth. Her breathing is shallow and fast. Like this.

Two and Three breathe shallow and fast.

Two I kneel beside her. I place my hand on the nape of her neck to comfort her. I look up, and for a moment I see Anna Bella Eema peering from the tattered curtains of the trailer home. The officer with the stun gun comes up to me.

Three Alright, now we got to take her to the hospital. Little girl? Little girl? That was a close one. We just saved your life.

Two And they take her away from me on a stretcher, but not before I take away a present. A reminder. A charm. When I take my hand off the nape of her neck, there was something in my fist.

Two opens up her fist. She has a handful of thick fur.

Fur.

Three
    EEEE-LEEEE
    AAAA-BAAA
    BAAA-AAAA
    LAAA-EEEEE
    NAAA-NAAA
    BAAA-BAAA
    EEEM-MAAA.

Two They put my mother into the hospital.
    They put the trailer home into a junk yard.
    They put me into a house with family named Currimpaw.
    There are two other kids and a swimming pool. They are nice.

The junkyard people refuse to junk the trailer home. They say 'Something is wrong with that trailer home.' They won't go inside, and the trailer home sits.
    Mother is not waking up.
    They tell me it's in my best interest to stay away.

And so that night, I climb through the window over the kitchen sink, and whoosh!

I am by my mother's side.

Mother is not waking up.

I walk up to the nurse's desk, and demand to know what is going on.

Two speaks to a nurse.

I demand to know what is going on!

Three Well, it has been six days, and we are trying our best. These things take time. She is still very strong. Her vital signs are, mmm – stable.

Two I want my mother back.

Three Well, sweetheart, the police will get her first. She seriously injured three officers, and one perfectly good construction worker. One of those men can't see now out of his right eye.

Two Will they put her away for a long time?

Three Sweetheart, *three officers*. In broad daylight. That means life.

Two In prison?

Three Sugar, don't you worry. They'll put her in a special hospital. She won't hurt anyone any more. Not even herself.

Two I am walking down the bright white hospital hallway. I am looking in the window of my mother's door. She is lying on the hospital bed, hands crossed across her chest, like she was already dead.

One sits up, eyes closed, hands crossed across her chest.

Her breathing is the same: shallow and fast.

One, Two and Three breathe shallow and fast. One

and Two continue as Three speaks.

Three Three policemen in broad daylight. That means *life*.

Three goes back to breathing as Two speaks.

Two Have the wild things no moral or legal rights? What right has man to inflict such long and fearful agony on a fellow creature, simply because that creature does not speak his language? All that day she hung on. Once a wolf, now a wounded partridge, she beats her great, strong wings, in helpless struggle to be free.

One and Two breathe shallow and slow as Three speaks.

Three Her vital signs are, mmm – stable.

One and Three breathe shallow and slow as Two speaks.

Two The morning broke, the day wore on, and still she hung there, slowly dying; her very strength a curse. The next night crawled slowly on, and in the dawdling hours of darkness, a great horned owl, drawn by the feeble flutter of a dying wing, cut short the pain, and the deed was wholly kind.

Three (*sings*)
    The blue iris,
    sign of the fool-crow
    sign of the ever-hopeful crow
    is fading from my eye
    I am growing fierce as time itself
    I am growing wild and all-knowing
    like a horned owl I am near you
    even when you don't want me near you.

    I am only ten years old
    this is the burden I carry
    to be wise as the sky itself
    I carry all this danger

I carry all this revolution
and I am only ten years old.

*As Three sings, Two goes to One and puts her mouth
on her neck as though she was a vampire, and begins
sucking the life out of her mother.*

I am only ten years old
I make the fox run
And the wolf cry
What's a girl to do with this kind of knowledge
What's a girl to do with this kind of pain
I make the fox run
And the wolf cry
I'm feeling so alive now.

One breathes her last breath.

Two Whirr, and up she went, a beautiful, sentient, noble
being.

*Pause. One stands up. One leaves the stage. Two takes
One's chair.*

None of the doctors know exactly what caused my
mother's death. They say one moment her heart was
beating strong and fast, and the next moment, it wasn't.
    A lion shorn of his strength, an eagle robbed of his
freedom, or a dove bereft of his mate all die, it is said, of
a broken heart.
    And then Nurse stands before me.

Two holds up a flip phone.

Anna Bella, your mom's on the phone.

One What?

Two Oh well, Mrs Curripaw. Your new mom? Is she –

Two Here.

It is as though Two grabbed the phone from the nurse.
Two has a phone in her hand. She flips it open. She
turns it in several directions. It is foreign to her.

New mom.
Newmom.
Momnewmom.

Two clicks the phone shut.

On the day I went to school for the first time in my entire
life, I hear two ladies whisper.

Three (*whispers, playing two parts*)
She spent her first ten years in a trailer park.
Really?
Her mother was crazy.
What is she now?
Dead.
Oh, poor thing.
Doomed, yes, but really quite sweet.
She has the most exotic set of eyes . . .

Two I do well in school, to everyone's surprise. They
imagine I will be unruly. What they forget is that the wild
creature's first and most important means of self-defence
is its ability to adapt.
    I miss my mother. She is extraordinarily gone. Only
her books remain. I read them all, twice, and then I bring
them to the library and donate them to their collection.
My 'new mom' does not think this is wise. But I want to
limit my possessions. I plan to travel some day.
    Many, many, many weeks after I moved into my new
home and started school, I was visted by Anna Bella
Eema, the little girl I made that day out of plain earth
behind the trailer home. I was lying in my bed, looking at
my laptop, when I heard a rapping on my window pane.
I had an instinctual knowledge of who it was. I closed the
computer, opened the window, and Anna Bella Eema

crawled into bed with me. It felt good, even though she was, of course, very very, muddy. I held her close to my chest. She nestled her muddy nose into my now-plump breasts. She made me laugh out loud.

Two laughs out loud.

Then she looked deep into my eyes, touched her nose to my nose, and said:

Three One. Two. Three.

Two And then she laughed out loud.

Three laughs out loud.

And I took my right hand, and touched my fingers to her lips.

Three stops laughing.

And reached up and closed both of her eyelids, and she was gone.

Three leaves the stage. Two takes a moment to consider the audience.

Here we are.

Some days I feel I am completely new. I have killed many things, and seen many new places. And other days, quiet days, I become very aware of my little-bird soul, still fluttering around in the cage of my ribs. The same little bird that the fox saw so clearly, the same little bird my mother felt fluttering in her womb. The same little bird that sprouted these fine white teeth.

She bares her teeth.

Highway 20 now cuts right through the heart of town. The speed limit is sixty miles per hour. It takes approximately three seconds to drive over the square of land that once was our trailer park. It's like it was never even there.

She takes out a small tape recorder. She looks at the audience.

She holds up fingers on her right hand, counting in silence.

Index finger (one), second finger (two), third finger (three).

She presses play. The sounds of an interstate highway fill the stage.

Two leaves the stage.

The sound continues for some time, until the interstate sounds vaguely like the crashing of waves. Darkness. Silence.

End of play.